Beginner's Guide to
Machine Embroidered
Landscapes

To my family who continue to
support and encourage me:
husband John, sons Thomas and
Jonathan, mum Brenda
and sister Pauline, thank you.

Beginner's Guide to
Machine Embroidered
Landscapes

SEARCH PRESS

First published in Great Britain 2001

Search Press Limited
Wellwood, North Farm Road,
Tunbridge Wells, Kent TN2 3DR

Reprinted 2003

ISBN 0 85532 917 3

The publishers and author can accept no responsibility for any
consequences arising from the information, advice or instructions
given in this publication.

Suppliers
Many of the threads used in this book are available from:
Madeira Threads (UK) Ltd., York Road, Thirsk, North Yorkshire
YO7 3BX

If you have difficulty in obtaining any of the materials and
equipment mentioned in this book, please visit the Search Press
website at **www.searchpress.com** for details of suppliers.
Alternatively, you can write to the publishers at the address above
for a current list of stockists, including firms which operate a mail-
order service.

Publisher's note
All the step-by-step photographs in this book feature the
author, Alison Holt, demonstrating how to create machine
embroidered gardens and landscapes. No models have
been used.

Printed in Spain by Elkar S. Coop, 48180 Loiu (Bizkaia)

I would like to thank everyone at Search Press
for their enthusiasm and help, especially Ally.
   Thanks also to my friends and students for
their generous support and encouragement.
   My gratitude to Madeira Threads (UK) Ltd
for the machine embroidery threads.
   Last, but not least, thank you to my family
who are simply wonderful.

Front cover *Embroidery based on a garden designed by Nikki
Bennett-Jane for the Chelsea Flower Show
size: 215 x 270mm (8½ x 10½ in)*

Page 1 Wild Flowers
Actual size

Page 3 Autumn Walk
size 230 x 140mm (9 x 5½ in)

Contents

Astilbe
size: 64 x 192mm (2½ x 7½ in)

Introduction

Machine embroidery is an extremely versatile medium: it is easy to achieve wonderful effects of colour and texture with thread. In this book I will show you how to develop your skills and begin to create beautiful embroideries on your machine.

I first started experimenting with fabric, thread and the sewing machine in the late 1970s. My final year at college was spent working with vanishing muslin, creating collage landscapes full of winter trees. I coloured silk using a dye bath and cut it up to make my collages. Painting colours directly on to the silk instead of using pieces of material was a natural progression, and since then, my way of working has evolved into a technique of 'painting' with threads.

I have been teaching textiles and embroidery for twenty years, and am as enthusiastic about machine embroidery as ever. The creative possibilities are endless, and in terms of scale and style of working, there is something for everyone. My loyal and enthusiastic students have always given me a great deal of encouragement, and I feel that at times I have gained as much from them as I hope they have from me.

At first, many people mistake my embroideries for paintings or even photographs. I am fascinated by gardens, landscapes and detail and enjoy the challenge of interpreting all the elements I see in nature. Inspiration is everywhere – in the effects of light on the landscape and in the juxtaposition of the amazing array of colours and textures in trees, foliage, flowers and plants.

I use two basic stitches: straight stitch and zigzag stitch, to make fine and broad brush strokes on a hand-painted silk surface, blending both to achieve different effects. The raised embroidery on the coloured background produces a beautiful three-dimensional effect.

When I first started to paint directly on the silk background, I also began to take photographs instead of sketching. I like to observe detail and colour and analyse form at the embroidery stage, so I work directly on to the fabric using the photograph or photographs as reference – I am actually drawing with the needle. If you are at all worried about working straight on to the fabric, it can be helpful to make a sketch first and work from this, breaking it up into several stages.

Many beginners lack confidence in their ability to draw, but even this is less of a problem than you might think. Machine embroidery has a life of its own and some wonderful effects can be achieved without particular drawing skills. You could start by simply placing an image under the silk and tracing key elements of the design. As your confidence grows, you will find it much easier to cut out this stage and begin to draw straight on to your fabric before stitching.

I would love to take my sewing machine and sit embroidering in the middle of the garden or landscape in which I find my inspiration, but there are too many practical difficulties. This is why I find photography the ideal solution. I choose my location, then take a large number of photographs, combining or cropping them to form a base or starting point for my designs.

A word of warning: work cautiously, and experiment with different techniques as you go along, as machine embroidery can be very difficult and time-consuming to unpick. Keep some fabric stretched in a spare hoop, and use it to practise techniques before working them on your picture. Make sure the colour, length and direction of the stitches are all you need them to be for the effect you are trying to create. Finally – and most importantly of all – enjoy it!

Two Chairs

The inspiration for this embroidery came from one of the gardens at the annual Hampton Court Palace Flower Show. The chairs were embroidered in zigzag stitch, a technique which stands out well against the texture of the gravel which is worked in running stitch.

Actual size

Materials & equipment

Machine embroidery

Sewing machine

Freehand or creative machine embroidery can be done on any electric sewing machine. A machine with a swing needle which does straight stitch and zigzag is best, as it will enable you to create more textures – see pages 43-52. A stitch width control dial is better than push buttons as it will give you a smooth increase in width and enable you to 'draw'. If you can remove the bobbin case on your machine, it will be easier to alter the tension screw.

Only a few simple changes are needed to adapt a machine for embroidery. The presser foot, which normally holds the fabric flat as it is guided under the needle, should be removed so that you can move the embroidery in any direction. The feed dog, which feeds the fabric through the machine and is linked with the stitch length control, should be lowered so you can move your embroidery at varying speeds and in any direction. This will give you different lengths of stitch: if you move your embroidery slowly you will make small stitches and if you move it quickly the stitches will be larger.

Fabric

There is a huge range of silk fabric. I use 8mm Habutai silk, a medium-weight silk with a fine weave and smooth appearance, ideal for the painted areas and the scale of the stitches in my embroideries. Lightweight cotton is a good substitute if you want to experiment before starting a design.

Threads

Machine embroidery threads are made especially for use with a machine and have a beautiful sheen. You will need a good selection of threads, but if you have done some machine embroidery, you may already have started a collection. I recommend that you not only increase your range, but add tones of the same colours. I use fine, pure cotton threads in soft natural colours. To provide a wider colour range, I also use threads in good quality cotton or poly-cotton mixes.

Needles

A wide variety of needles is available, and I find size 80 (12) ideal for the weight of silk I use.

Embroidery hoop

Fabric should be stretched in a hoop to keep it flat and prevent puckering or distortion. Stretch it very tightly so there is no give as you are working; if it is held too loosely, the machine may miss stitches and the thread will fray and eventually break. A hoop with a slotted screw which can be tightened with a screwdriver will maintain a really good tension. I use a 20cm (8in) wooden embroidery hoop and bind the inner ring with woven tape, to give a better grip on the fabric and prevent it from being marked.

Screwdrivers

You will need a small screwdriver to adjust the tension on the bobbin case and a larger one to tighten the screw on the hoop.

Embroidery scissors

Make sure these are comfortable to use, with sharp, pointed ends so you will be able to cut threads close to the work on the right side of your embroidery.

Bobbins

Have plenty of spare bobbins so you can keep a range of colours wound ready for use.

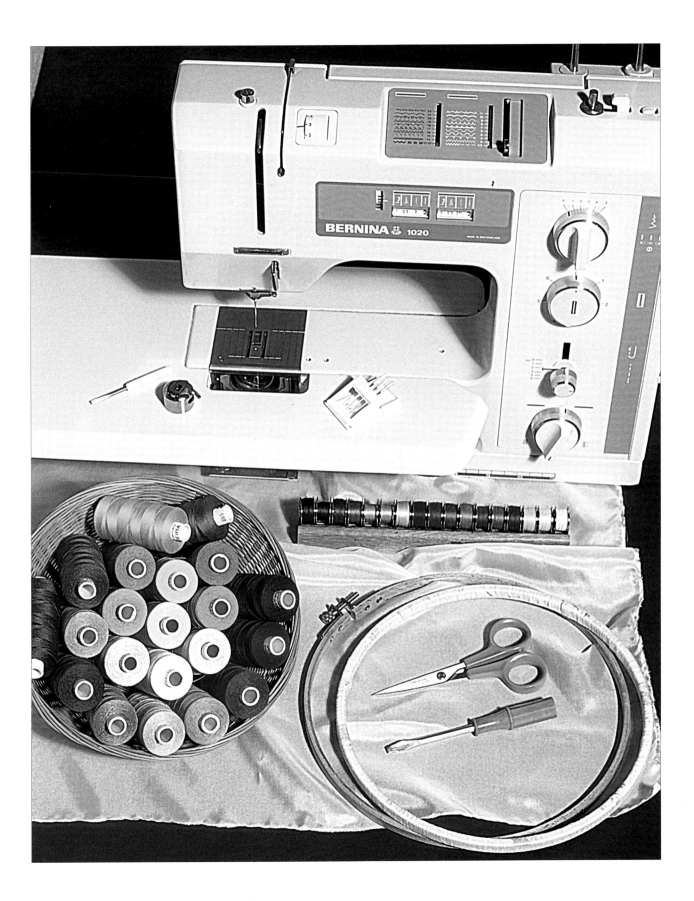

Silk painting

Before starting to embroider, I stretch the silk on a frame, then paint in the main elements of my design. All materials listed here are readily available from good art or craft shops.

Silk dyes

I prefer dyes to fabric paints, because dyes change only the colour, not the appearance, of the fabric. Paint tends to sit on the surface of the silk, which spoils the sheen. I use water-based dyes which are suitable for silk, cotton and synthetic fabrics. They are available in a wide range of colours and are easy to fix with a hot iron. The colours can be used directly from the bottle; mixed together to make new colours or made paler by adding water.

Resist (outliner)

This is a clear gel which dries to form a barrier between different areas of dye and is used to control the flow of the dyes on the silk. Transfer it to a small pipette, with a nib attached to the nozzle, and use to define your design into areas of colour. A No.6 nib is ideal, as it produces lines which are fine enough for my designs but will still contain the dyes.

Wooden frame

The silk should be stretched on a frame when applying dyes. An embroidery hoop can be used, but this will restrict the size of your design image. I use a frame 40cm (16in) square. This allows me to paint one large image, or several smaller images.

Silk pins

These are pins which have three small prongs and grip the fabric better than an ordinary drawing pin. They are also less likely to tear the fabric.

Palette

I always use a ceramic palette because dyes tend to discolour the plastic variety. White is best, so you can see the colours you are mixing.

Paintbrushes

For painting on fine silk, I use good quality watercolour brushes in a range of sizes: Nos. 000, 0, 2 and 5. The small brushes are ideal for fine details and the larger size for washes of colour.

Water/air-soluble pen

Use this to trace the design on to the fabric, or to mark out details of the composition after painting.

Hairdryer

This can be used to dry the outliner so you can move more quickly to the painting stage. It will also dry the dye quickly and prevent it spreading too far.

Craft knife

Use this to cut the end of the nozzle on the pipette.

Tracing paper

This can be used to trace the design on to silk by marking it out and placing it under the fabric.

Marker pen

Use a black pen to mark a design on tracing paper so it will show strongly through the silk.

Rule

This is useful for giving your picture straight edges and for ensuring that it is square.

Iron

This is used to fix the silk dyes to the silk, and for ironing dry the wet silk after washing out the resist.

Pipette

A small plastic bottle, with a nozzle which can be cut to take a nib, for use with resist.

Nib

A metal nib will give you more control over the line of resist when drawing your design.

Design

This always the first stage. It can be daunting for someone who is not used to composing their own pictures and designs, but it is not as difficult as you might think. If you look, inspiration is everywhere.

I find my inspiration in flowers, gardens and the countryside and I love to translate what I see into a combination of painted backgrounds and beautiful textured stitches.

What makes a successful design or composition? The answer is simple: whatever works visually for you because we all have an innate sense of design.

We are attracted to a scene by the shapes and colours we see in it. Deciding where to place them in your composition is the first step toward design.

Designs should have a *focal point*, an area of interest to which the eye is drawn before taking in the rest of the picture. Designs should incorporate shapes in the composition which lead the eye from one area to another. All principles of design can be considered when looking through the camera lens or cropping a photograph.

Herb garden
This design works well with the smooth, painted path which contrasts with the textured foliage of the borders. There is a rhythm in the repetition of the topiary spheres, leading the eye into the distance.
Actual size

Composition

Composing a picture involves arranging the elements of shape, colour and texture to create harmony within a structure. Think about the dimensions of your design: it could be a square, circle, rectangle or an oval. There are many theories of design, but for a successful design consideration should be given to the following:

Contrast
This can be achieved with textures such as rough and smooth, shiny and matt or hard and soft; tonal contrasts using light and dark, or by using complementary colours: red and green; purple and yellow or orange and blue. Consider also the use of contrasting shapes within your design.

Rhythm
This can be created by repetition, such as the use of waves of poppies in a field or of bluebells in a wood. The repetition of the same shape or colour along the length of a flower border is another way in which you can use this principle of design. It gives a natural order to the composition.

Negative shapes
The shapes between the positive elements in the composition are also significant, and should be given consideration to ensure that all parts of the design are of equal importance.

The Golden Section

Many of my designs, including *Bluebell Walk,* below, are based on the principle of the Golden Section, which relates to the idea of balance in an asymmetrical composition.

The basic idea behind the principle is that we have a natural tendency to divide a rectangle or a line in the proportion of approximately one-third: two-thirds. This can be used to determine where the focal point is placed; the proportions of the colours used, or the position of the horizon. We will be comfortable with this natural balance. This holds true whether you are dealing with colour, the alignment of the horizon or the position of a focal point.

The theory of the Golden Section should be considered when you are beginning to design, but remember if you are happy with the way your design looks – even if it does not follow any recognised guidelines – you should go with your instincts.

Bluebell Walk
*The composition of this picture is a good example
of the principle of the Golden Section.*

Actual size

13

Using photographs

Sketching or painting is a thoroughly enjoyable way of recording what you see. It is also time-consuming, so I have developed my photography skills with the help of a camera which has automatic focus and exposure. This means I can concentrate on the composition of my picture, and let the camera take care of the details.

My drawing and painting skills are integral to the work I produce, but for anyone lacking an artistic background there are short-cuts. Many of my students take their inspiration from wonderful collections of magazine cuttings, postcards and birthday cards. You should remember, however, that if you do want to copy a printed image, the permission of the copyright holder must be sought.

I compose my embroideries as I look through the lens of my camera. Back in the studio, I apply the design directly to the silk. It is at this stage that I seek to recapture the atmosphere and the strong visual elements which first attracted me to the scene.

Photographs can be used entire, or cropped to create a better composition. Another way to produce an effective design is to use several photographs of the same scene, taking details from each in order to achieve exactly the effect you want. The following pages illustrate these ideas.

The embroidery

Using one photograph for the composition and others for details can work well. The yellow irises add interest and give the embroidery a better compositional balance, enhanced because purple is yellow's complementary colour.
Size: 127 x 174mm (5 x 7in)

Above and right
source photographs

14

Azalea garden

I took a photograph of this garden (see right), and did not need to alter the composition in any way. As there is a wealth of detail I scaled up the design which created enough space for the embroidery techniques. Emphasising the colourful azaleas and the bright, yellow-green leaves of spring lends a vibrancy to the finished embroidery.

source photograph

The embroidery

Soft lines were painted on the neatly-cut lawn with a No.000 brush and a small amount of dye. To create a feeling of depth the distant trees were embroidered with a small straight stitch. The azalea flowers, the leaves on the foreground tree and the hostas are worked in zigzag, a larger-scale stitch which makes these elements seem closer.

Size: 230 x 140mm (9 x 5½ in)

Cropping

Effective cropping can add an extra dimension to your composition, helping to create the atmosphere you want the finished work to reflect. For example, framing your composition with a square or oval will help to create an intimate feel, while cropping it vertically can help to emphasise a vertical element of your design such as tall delphiniums.

Cropping also enables you to focus on just one element of a picture, eliminating unwanted sections and improving the composition. Experiment by moving two L-shaped pieces of card over your photograph, framing different sections until you achieve a pleasing effect.

The original photograph has the gate as a focal point and white flowers spreading across approximately one-third of the composition.

The photograph, cropped to focus on the area of interest.

The completed embroidery with poppies added to the foreground to provide extra visual interest.

Laburnum arch

I cropped this photograph on each side and extended the base to create an elongated composition. This emphasises the tunnel effect and draws the eye into the distance, adding to the depth of the picture. I think this is a more elegant format than the photograph, and it evokes the feel of the laburnum arch as I remember it.

The embroidery
Shadows are painted on the pathway, creating a quiet area which contrasts with the busy arch. The rhythm of the trunks and branches of the laburnum leads the eye into the picture.

Actual size

Cow parsley

Cropping makes a dramatic difference to this composition. I was drawn to the spray of cow parsley in the centre of this scene, but its impact is diminished by the rest of the view.

Cropping horizontally allows me to remove the unwanted elements of the photograph, especially the lower part which lacks detail and interest, and focus more on the cow parsley.

source photograph

The source photograph after cropping. The horizon is one-third down, and the hedge is one-third in from the edge of the picture.

The embroidery
The cow parsley has been given more emphasis than in the photograph, with its textured heads contrasting effectively with the painted sky.
Actual size

18

Topiary and alliums

The photograph I took of this view (below left) presents a perfectly pleasing composition, but I was particularly interested in the spiral topiary and wanted to make it a feature of my embroidery. A close vertical crop has brought the tree into greater prominence, as well as helping to emphasise its height. Accentuating the difference in the colour of the greenery has also increased the focus on the tree.

Source photograph

The embroidery
Actual size

19

Foxglove garden

Cropping this photograph has changed its proportions and emphasised the vertical element created by the foxgloves.

The camera I use gives only two choices when framing a composition, portrait or landscape, but no choice about proportions. Cropping means I do not have to accept what the camera gives me: I can consider the elements in the picture and enhance them.

Selecting this section of the foxglove garden emphasises the height of the flowers yet retains other areas of interest, such as the terracotta sphere painted in the foreground which echoes and forms a link with the brickwork in the distance.

Source photograph

Finished embroidery
Actual size

Two trees

The source photograph for this embroidery was cropped to divide the composition vertically into three sections – see the Golden Section, page 12. The horizontal branches and foliage create a rhythm, continued by the band of distant trees, wire fence and stone wall.

Actual size

Combining photographs

I often take many photographs of a scene: close-ups of different areas for detail and colour reference, and several overviews for composition ideas. This enables me to get a good 'feel' about the subject when I am deciding on my final design back in the studio. This embroidery of honeysuckle is a good example.

To combine all the photographs for the final image, I first decided what size and shape I wanted the finished embroidery to be, which in this case was 128 x 280mm (5 x 11in). These proportions allow space for the two strong linear features: the tall post in the foreground and the silver birch trees in the distance.

I placed the post in the composition so that it would occupy one-third of the vertical space. The other elements of the picture were fitted around it to create a balance.

The foliage of the silver birch trees was embroidered in a small straight stitch, moving the hoop slowly with a restricted spiralling motion to give stitches lying in all directions. Seven shades of green were used, starting with the darkest tone and working through to the highlight. The trunks were embroidered with pale grey on top and dark grey in the bobbin, using a closely-worked zigzag stitch decreasing gradually in width towards the top.

The small pink flowers in the shadows at the base of the tree were achieved by putting pink in the bobbin and dark green on top, tightening the top tension to pull the bobbin thread to the surface and give flecks of pink within the dark area.

The fern and honeysuckle leaves were worked in a zigzag stitch of varying width, by moving the hoop slowly with one hand while altering the dial controlling the stitch width with the other. For fern, the width of the stitch was decreased gradually, while for the honeysuckle the width was increased to the centre of the leaf, then decreased to create the shape. The flowers are a combination of zigzag stitch and straight stitch.

The photographs show several views of the same scene, highlighting the different elements that I wanted to include in my finished composition.

The embroidery

Areas of interest include the painted post, and the use of zigzag for the ferns and the honeysuckle leaves.

size: 128 x 280mm (5 x 11in)

A sense of scale

One way in which combining photographs can prove particularly effective is to help to give a sense of scale to your composition.

When you stand in a field of poppies, the sheer immensity of the landscape and the feeling of oneness with nature can be overwhelming. The problem of how to recreate that feeling can be overcome by using a panoramic view, combining two or more images if necessary.

In this embroidery of a poppy-filled cornfield, the long, narrow format complements the sweeping vastness of the expanse of corn and emphasises the absence of any human element. The pylon has been removed for aesthetic reasons.

The photographs were overlapped to create one image.

Poppies and corn

Poppies were added to create more foreground interest. The cornfield occupies two-thirds of the picture.

Size: 255 x 76mm (11 x 3in)

Two photographs of my own garden
have been joined for this
composition, which divides into
roughly two-thirds lawn and one-
third distant border. I took the
foreground shot, then moved my
camera carefully on the vertical to
photograph the distance.

Here there is a balance between the
busy-textured flower border and the
calm green lawn which is
predominantly painted.
Size: 127 x 305mm (5 x 12in)

Colour

Colour should be used in your design to create contrast, focus and impact. Complementary colours – for example blue and orange, red and green or purple and yellow, when they are used together, create impact.

Perception of a colour is influenced by its surroundings: a colour will appear brighter or duller in comparison with those next to it. A red poppy seen in green grass will appear more intense because green and red are complementary colours, though this works to best effect only when the red and green are of the correct hue. Experiment with the proportions of each colour you use, and do not forget there are times when a single poppy can create more impact than a field full.

colours shown are dyes direct from the bottle

26

Mixing colour

Mixing the colour of dye you want to paint with can be difficult at first, but understanding the basic rules of colour theory makes it easier to see how colours are achieved.

You may be familiar with the colour wheel showing variations of the three *primary* colours: red, blue and yellow. If a primary colour is mixed with another primary colour the result is a *secondary* colour i.e. orange, purple and green. When a primary colour is mixed with a secondary colour the result is a *tertiary* colour.

An idea which can prove more useful than the traditional colour wheel is a colour grid (see opposite). This shows all the dyes *you* have and the colours they will produce when mixed in equal quantities with each other. A grid can be a good point of reference when you first try to mix a colour to paint on the silk background. Completing your own grid will help you understand how to achieve a range of colours with the dyes you have at hand and create your own palette.

Using the colour grid

The main grid is designed to help you to mix colours in your palette.

Choose the colour you would like to achieve from your grid. Then simply follow the squares down to the bottom and across to the diagonal to identify the two dye colours you will need to mix it. Test the shade on a spare piece of silk and add water to make the colour lighter in tone if necessary.

Varying the tones

You can go on from the grid to achieve more colours by varying the quantities of dye and the number of colours mixed together.

To make colours lighter in tone just add water - the second grid (above) shows the effect of different quantities of water on the dye. Adding more water to each colour will help you to become aware of how the dyes change.

Preparing resist

Resist is applied to dry fabric, and allowed to dry before painting begins. I use a small plastic pipette and a size 6 metal nib, which helps to control the flow of resist and gives a fine line.

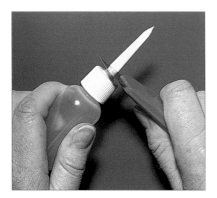

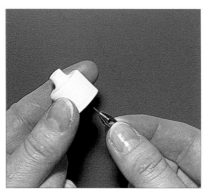

1. Cut off the nozzle of the pipette just above the cap as shown.

2. Push the nib through the cap from behind until it fits securely. Fill the pipette with resist and replace the cap.

Note
Store the resist upright, with the wire inserted in the nib, to prevent blockages.

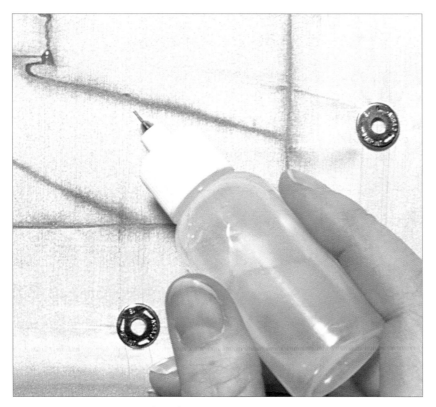

Keep an even pressure on the nib when applying resist. Make sure the resist is dry before you start to paint.

Using resist

Wherever you draw with resist a white line will be left, so it can help to think of it as a white pen.

Keep the number of lines you draw to a minimum, breaking the design down into simple blocks of colour. To ensure even lines, keep the pressure on your pipette constant as you apply resist. The skill is in balancing the amount of pressure you put on the pipette and the speed at which you move it, to create a smooth line with a consistent width.

Hold the pipette like a pencil and squeeze it gently as you move over the design. If there is any leakage, tape up the join between the nib and the nozzle.

To check that a line of resist has been applied effectively, hold your design up to the light to make sure there are no breaks.

Blue hosta

Resist was used to good effect in this picture. The pots and individual leaves of the hosta were outlined to prevent the dye spreading when painting. The painted detail on the main pot was built up with a small brush, layering colour on colour and letting the dye dry each time. The embroidered areas were extended to cover the white outlines left round the shapes by the resist.

Actual size

Painted backgrounds

Decisions about which parts of your picture to embroider and which to paint are made after studying the source photograph. Textured details like foliage, flowers, gravel and stones should be embroidered, and a simple wash of dye in an appropriate colour is enough to form the base of these areas. Areas with detail but not texture – the smooth or shiny elements in a composition – are better painted. These could include reflections in water, paving, or shadows on a flat surface, all of which provide contrast in the composition. The painting I do as a base for my embroideries can be broken up into three types: blocking in colour; painting a wash and painting detail.

Blocking in colour

This is the base for embroidery or textured detail. It will be covered entirely in stitch, so only a simple wash in a suitable colour is needed: mid-green for a field, or mid-brown for a cornfield – see page 32.

Painting with silk dye is similar to painting with watercolour, except that the dye spreads more on fabric than paint does on paper. To control the flow of the dye you must use the correct size of brush for the area you are trying to paint. Key elements of a composition are outlined with *resist* (see page 28), which forms a barrier and prevents colours running into each other on the silk. You will then be able to paint within the outline formed by the resist.

Wherever resist is used it will leave a white line, so it must be used sparingly. To disguise resist, you should plan to cover it with embroidery. Remember that this will increase the size of the shape you are outlining; compensate by reducing the size of the area slightly at the drawing stage.

If you are unsure about drawing straight on to your silk with resist, it is a good idea to trace the main elements of your source photograph. Use a black marker pen to do this, and you should find it easy to lay your silk over the tracing paper and go over the outlines with air- or water-soluble pen.

When painting within an outline, keep the brush stroke 0.5cm (¼ in) away from the line of resist and let the dye flood up to it to create blocks of colour.

The painted background
Simple washes of colour have been used for the textured area of foliage. The reflections, the lily pads and the stones by the water's edge have been painted in detail.

The source photograph

The traced outline

Iris and waterlilies
Actual size

Painting a wash

This technique is for an area where little or no stitching will be added, for example simple skies or as the background colour for a wall on which only the mortar will be stitched. A wash of green shaded from light to dark is ideal as the base for a lawn which will include just a small amount of stitch – see page 13, *Blue Border*.

Resist should be used to separate areas of wash only when the white line it leaves can be covered by embroidery. The example below shows a simple wash for a shaded sky. I mixed and tested all the paint I needed before I began: this means that you can work quickly without having to worry about whether you can obtain the right shade for the next section. Three shades were all I needed to blend the sky from pale blue at the bottom to mid-blue at the top. I rarely paint sky in any more detail, as in my embroideries it is usually covered by trees or foliage. The area of grass and the cornfield are simply blocked in with colour.

Simple background wash technique

Using a No.5 brush and starting at the base of the sky with the palest blue, make one slow, horizontal brush stroke straight across the picture. Repeat the process with the mid-toned blue, overlapping the brush strokes slightly across the first. Change to the third and deepest shade of blue and add the final brush stroke to finish the area of sky.

Complete the area of field next, using a No.5 brush and one shade of yellow ochre. Use a smaller brush (No.0) to add the tiny areas of green and yellow for the distant foliage. Finally, complete the foreground area of foliage as for the sky but using three different shades of green. Leave to dry.

When rinsing your brush to change colours, squeeze out the excess water with your fingers, or dry the brush with a paper towel. This will prevent the dye being diluted and making the colours too pale.

Do not wash out the brush when you change tones within a colour range as this helps to blend them. You must work quickly, as the effect depends on the dyes being wet on the silk. If the dye is allowed to dry between applications, there will be a hard line where the different tones meet.

Always test the dye before applying, as when it dries it will look lighter. I usually use the area of silk around the margin of the picture to test colours.

Painting detail

This is for areas which will have no embroidery added, so the painting provides the detail. It is used for areas with little or no texture, like reflections on water, smooth terracotta pots or shadows on a path.

When your embroidery is complete, some of the painted areas may not look strong enough tonally. Do not worry, as more dye can be applied later to correct the balance of the composition.

Choosing brushes

The size of brush affects the control you have over the dye. For a flat colour wash in a less-detailed area (for example sky), use a larger brush such as a No.5, which holds a lot of dye and helps to reduce the risk of lines or streaks. If you want the dye colours to blend into each other, apply another colour before the previous colour has dried.

For small areas and fine details, use a small brush (000, 0 or 1) and just a little dye. Experiment with different sizes of brush on a spare piece of silk by making a brush stroke and seeing how far it spreads. This will give you a good idea of the size of brush you will need for each individual area contained by resist. If you use too much dye it may break through the line of resist or spread too far.

Another way to control the dye is by letting one colour dry before adding the next, which makes the silk less absorbent and stops the dye spreading. This is ideal for separate colours and fine lines of dye. Begin with the palest tone and build up layers of dye through the tones, ending with the darkest. Let each colour dry thoroughly before applying the next. A hairdryer will speed up the process.

> ### Note
> If you use air-soluble pen to draw your design, wait for it to disappear before beginning to embroider. If you do not do this, the ink from the air-soluble pen may impede the flow of the dye.

Fern shadows
A pale wash was applied and allowed to dry, then the detail was painted on the boarded walkway with a small brush.

Actual size

Agapanthus at the Chelsea Flower Show
*The paving, water and foreground pot are all painted
areas. Straight stitch has been used to cover the white line
created by the resist at the edge of the paving. This gives
definition to the shape of the pond, while individual
paving stones are emphasised by stitching.*

Actual size

Terracotta pots

In this embroidery, only a simple wash was used behind the foliage, and I drew guide lines in outliner because I knew they would be covered in stitch. The pot at the top is a good example of painted detail: a pale wash of terracotta dye was applied and allowed to dry, then layers of progressively darker washes were applied with a small brush (No. 00) to create shading on the left side and under the rim. Each colour was allowed to dry before the next shade was added. The shadow of the grasses was painted last.

Actual size

Choosing threads

After investigating and experimenting with mixing dyes, choosing the coloured threads for your embroidery should prove a little easier. Identifying colours in your picture and matching them to the embroidery threads is the next stage.

I find that the best way to choose the right shade is to hold the reel of thread over a photograph, then look from the photograph to the reel and back again. Turning your photograph upside down when you are selecting the threads will prevent you from looking at the picture and enable you to focus on the colours alone. Make sure you are sitting in natural daylight for true colour matching.

I work by breaking down the elements of a photograph and analysing it in terms of colour, form and texture. The elements are reconstructed in paint and stitched to form a picture. Each section of the picture requires this process of visual dissection, so decisions can be made about what colour to paint the background, the colours of thread needed, and the length, direction and type of stitch needed to create the desired effect.

It is important to select colours in groups of tonal ranges. Start with the most distant area in the picture which will be the first area you embroider. Analyse how many shades or tones of the colour it will take to recreate the effect of that particular area. I find the best way to begin is to identify the deepest and lightest tones, then fill in the middle range.

The source photograph for the embroidery opposite, showing the threads selected to complete each area. Note the wide tonal range for each coloured section.

36

Rocky trail

The distant trees were completed first in a small straight stitch, followed by the moss and stones, in straight stitch following the slope of the bank. When the distant ground was complete the trees were added using vertical, parallel lines of straight stitch, shaded from light to dark to give form. The small trees were embroidered using lines of closely-worked zigzag, tapering to form narrow branches. For the foreground, the darkest tones were stitched first, then the mid-tones and finally the highlights. The lines of straight stitch describe the contours of the rocks and ground, making them seem three-dimensional.

Actual size·

The tonal range

One of the most common errors people make when selecting colours is to choose too limited a tonal range. It may sound obvious, but make sure that your dark shades are dark enough and your light shades light enough, or the finished piece will look flat and lack both depth and perspective.

When you have chosen your palette, make a note of which threads are intended for each area, or select small groups of threads, embroider with them and then move on to choose another group.

When selecting threads you need to train yourself to analyse colour accurately and to see the colours that are really there. We have preconceived ideas about what colour things are – for example that tree

trunks are brown and that leaves are green – but if you really look at your photograph, you are likely to find tree trunks in shades of grey and green rather than brown. Leaves can range from dark blue and grey, to almost white where there are highlights.

If you cannot match a colour from the photograph to a thread, you may be able to achieve the right visual effect by mixing two threads. I often do this in my embroideries, using one colour on the bobbin and another on top so that flecks of the bobbin colour show on the surface. This is similar to the impressionist painting technique of pointillism, in which dots of pure colour, when viewed from a distance, fuse into intermediate shades or tones.

Source photograph and threads

38

Oranges and Lemons

The garden in this photograph has a wealth of texture and colour, and the correct choice of colours is very important. Without the dark green in the distant foliage, there would not be a strong contrast with the yellow climber.

Laying out the threads in groups enables you to see if the tonal range is wide enough, and whether the colours look right together. It may sometimes be necessary to select a shade which is darker or lighter than in reality to obtain the right effect.

Actual size

Starting to embroider

Setting up your machine

A few small adjustments will be needed before you can use your machine for embroidery.

Remove the presser foot

This should unclip or unscrew from the base of the presser bar, and removing it gives you an unobstructed view of your embroidery. The presser foot usually keeps the fabric flat on the bed of the machine, but in machine embroidery the fabric is held flat by the hoop in which the fabric is stretched. Some manufacturers recommend using a darning or embroidery foot on the machine, but this is not necessary.

Lower the feed dog

This is usually done with a switch, and on some machines it is the same setting as for darning. If you cannot lower the feed dog, your machine may have a raised plate to fit over the moving teeth. If neither of these is possible, set the stitch length to 0. Each of these options will achieve the same result: the freedom to move your embroidery in any direction and at any speed.

Tension

When a sewing machine is used conventionally, the tension of the top and bobbin threads needs to be balanced to form the perfect stitch. With machine embroidery, you can create a variety of textures and effects by experimenting with the tension. To change the tension, and therefore the flow of thread from the bobbin, there is a tension screw on the bobbin case.

For a neat, flat stitch with the top thread but not the bobbin thread showing, turn the tension screw clockwise. This will tighten the tension and restrict the flow of the thread, which stops it showing on the surface of the fabric. This is ideal for fine detail.

For a stitch with a flecked effect which is ideal for blending and shading, use different colours of thread on top and in the bobbin. Turn the tension screw in an anti-clockwise direction, which will loosen the tension and allow the thread to flow more freely, so both the top and bobbin threads will be visible on the surface of the fabric.

The proportion of bobbin thread showing on the surface can be further increased by tightening the top tension, by turning the tension dial to a higher number or towards the '+' sign. This creates a highly-textured effect which, depending on how you move the hoop and whether the machine is set on straight or zigzag stitch, can be extremely versatile.

Preparing fabric for embroidering

Before you begin to embroider your fabric there are six steps to follow.

1. Draw your design on the stretched fabric with resist and allow it to dry
2. Paint with silk dyes and allow to dry.
3. Iron the fabric with a hot iron for two minutes to fix the dye to the fabric.
4. Wash the silk in hot, soapy water to remove the resist.
5. Rinse in clear water.
6. Iron your work dry to avoid creases in the silk.

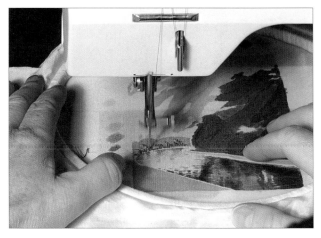

Making the first few stitches on prepared fabric

Making a start

Make sure you are sitting at the correct height for the machine. Rest your forearm or elbow on the table to give yourself a pivot point, which allows you more control over the movement of the hoop.

Stretch some lightweight cotton in a hoop, which will keep the fabric flat and prevent it becoming puckered or distorted. The hoop should be bound with cotton tape, which will help to grip the fabric and hold it secure. The hoop gives you something to hold when you are guiding the picture under the needle, and your fingers will be safe on or outside it. If the fabric starts to pucker or the machine misses stitches, stretch the fabric more tightly in the hoop.

Thread the machine with two different colours so you can see the effect of altering the tension. Pull the bobbin thread to the surface and hold both threads for the first few stitches to prevent knotting, then cut the tails off. Remember to lower the presser foot lever.

Hostas and foxgloves
This picture incorporates a wealth of stitch textures: straight stitch for the hosta leaves, variegated grass and fern; zigzag for the foxgloves and hosta flower petals

Carrying threads over

If you want to use the same colour in different areas of your picture, there is no need to cut the threads. When you have finished one section, take the thread across to where you want it by hand and place the needle in the new position. Turn the wheel by hand and anchor the thread with two or three stitches, then carry on embroidering. The trailing threads can be cut away later – see below for method.

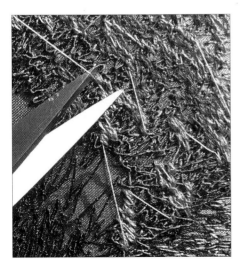

1. Slide the point of your scissors under the thread which has been carried across and snip it close to the surface of your work.

2. Pick up the loose end of thread between your thumb and forefinger and pull it taut, then snip it close to the surface of your work.

Shading and blending

The fruit pictures below have been worked using a simple shading technique which involves changing the top and bobbin threads independently of each other until the desired effect is achieved. Experiment until you can blend the shades of embroidery threads from dark to light or vice versa

Victoria Plums
Actual size

Bramley Apples
Actual size

Raspberries
Actual size

Simple technique for shading

This technique can be seen at its best in the example of the Victoria plums above. To make it easier, lay out each colour group of threads from the darkest to the lightest tones before you start to embroider. The following hints assume that you are using four tones, but the technique works with any number.

1. Thread the darkest shade (tone 1) on both the top and the bobbin and sew small parallel rows of straight stitch.
2. Change the top thread only to the next lighter shade (tone 2) and work the next section.
3. Change the bobbin thread to tone 2 and put the next lighter shade (tone 3) on top for the next area.
4. Put tone 3 in the bobbin and the lightest shade (tone 4) on top.

Changing and grading colours for shading works effectively when using straight stitch, with the top tension tightened slightly so the bobbin thread is visible. Embroidering a series of parallel lines works well for smooth objects, and a spiralling stitch gives more texture for foliage or gravel.

42

Stitch techniques

My embroideries are all worked in a combination of straight and zigzag stitches. Variations of each are achieved by changing the direction and speed at which the hoop is moved, and by altering the tension of the top and bobbin threads.

The length of straight stitch is influenced by the speed at which the hoop is moved: move it slowly to produce small stitches and quickly for longer stitches. Different hand movements also influence the result. Experiment by moving the hoop in parallel lines, in small circles or from side to side.

The appearance of zigzags is also changed by the speed and direction in which the hoop is moved. An advantage of zigzag stitch is that you have a choice of widths of 'line' to draw or experiment with. If you hold the hoop still you can build up, stitch by stitch, a machine embroidered 'French knot'.

When you add in the facility to change tension to these methods of varying the stitch, the range of marks and textures you can create is endless.

Analyse each element of your picture and decide the colour, direction and size of each stitch needed to create the effect you want. Experiment with straight or zigzag stitches, using a variety of hand movements and tensions, to see what you can achieve. Small stitches in the distance create a sense of scale, while larger stitches used in the foreground will give perspective to your work.

Azaleas

I was fascinated by the shapes of the trunks and branches of these azaleas. They are embroidered in closely-worked (with a slow movement of the hoop) zigzag stitch which narrows in width towards the top. The leaves are also zigzag, and are created by increasing the width of the stitch to the middle of the leaf, then decreasing it to the end. The fallen petals are zigzags worked on the spot, with straight stitch between them to cover the connecting thread.

Actual size

Experimenting with straight stitch

Straight stitch is best for the finer details in an embroidery and is always used in the distance of a picture. Exciting textures can be created with a tight top tension and a loose bottom tension.

If you want to blend a colour with the embroidery, use different tones on top and in the bobbin. For a colour or stitch line which will stand out well, use the same colour on top and in the bobbin.

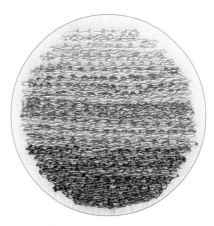

A spiralling straight stitch worked horizontally is effective for a gravel path. The tight top tension pulls up the darker bottom thread.

Parallel lines close together and several colour changes give a shaded effect for tree trunks. The different colours on top and in the bobbin to assist blending. This technique can also be used for fruit or pots (see apple, page 42).

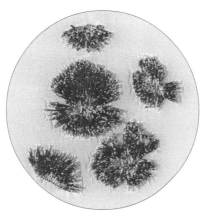

For flower petals with closely-worked parallel lines using a tight top tension. Using a light colour in the bobbin gives a highlight at the edge of the petal.

A spiralling straight stitch worked in a cone shape is ideal for laburnum.

For rocks or boulders, work parallel lines to follow the contours of the shape.

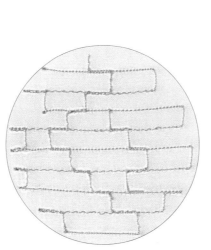

For mortar lines between bricks, work horizontal and vertical lines slowly to give small stitches, using the same colour on top and in the bobbin, and normal tension.

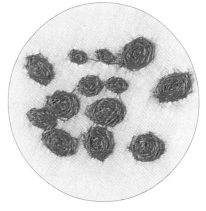

For flower heads like roses and peonies, move the hoop in small circles so that the stitches lie on top of the previous stitches. Work from the centre outwards.

For iris leaves, work parallel lines using the same colour on top and in the bobbin. Work dark tones first.

For ferns in the distance, work straight stitch with a slow movement of the hoop, using the same colour on the top and in the bobbin.

For foliage in a garden border, create vertical bands of diagonal stitches by moving your hand up and down slightly while moving the hoop vertically. Use a tighter top tension and a dark colour in the bobbin to help with blending.

For tree foliage in the middle distance, work a spiralling stitch, curving it to follow the line of the branches.

For grass, work varying lengths of vertical straight stitch, using the same colour on top and in the bobbin and normal tension, working the dark tones first.

The shading of foliage within bushes or trees is achieved by using different colours on top and in the bobbin. Work in a spiralling stitch overlapping each colour.

For hedgerows in the distance, move the hoop slowly to give tiny stitches, and work the dark colours first.

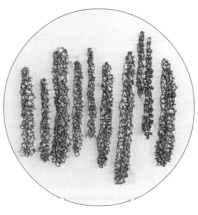

For delphiniums and other tall flowers, work spiralling straight stitch vertically. The technique is ideal for distant flowers where the colour and shape suggest the type of flower.

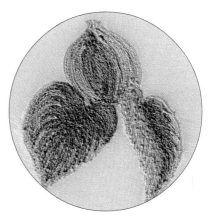

For large leaves in the foreground, like hostas, use straight stitch to fill in the shape and the same colour on top and in the bobbin.

Frosty Grasses

All the embroidery in this picture is straight stitch, showing the variety which can be achieved with different movements of the hoop. Direction and length of stitch are very important: a light touch is needed for the foreground grass which falls delicately over the lawn.

Actual size

Experimenting with zigzag stitch

Zigzag stitch is extremely versatile because it allows you to vary the width of your stitches for a wide range of different effects. Practise moving the hoop with one hand and altering the width of the zigzag with the other, which allows you to 'draw' with a line of varying width. The technique has many applications including flowers, leaves, tree trunks and branches.

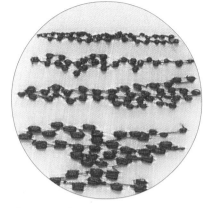

Flowers such as poppies or buttercups in a field at middle distance are worked using blocks of zigzag in a horizontal line.

For tree trunks work a single row for the distance, or use three overlapping rows in different tones to give a shaded effect if the tree is in the middle distance and seen in more detail. Use the same colour on top and in the bobbin.

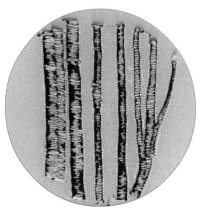

These tree trunks were worked with a slow movement so the stitches are very close together. A tight top tension and darker thread in the bobbin pulls up each side of trunk to form shading, making this effective for silver birch trees.

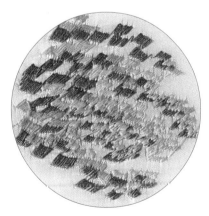

For these leaves, use normal tension to work zigzag in blocks, in a diagonal direction as if following the branch on the tree

For a tree, decrease the width of the zigzag as you move the hoop slowly to the top of the tree shape. The same colour has been used on top and in the bobbin.

For each trumpet of foxgloves, decrease the width of the zigzag towards the stem of the flower. Note that the trumpets increase in size towards the base of the foxglove.

These leaves are created by increasing and then decreasing the width of zigzag, and moving the hoop in a curve along the width of the leaf.

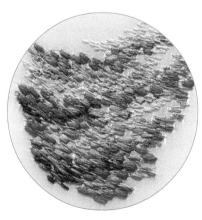

For autumn foliage, work drifts of zigzag on the spot, varying the size of the zigzag and creating a curved shape with each colour.

These leaves are created by varying the width of the zigzag from 0 to 5 and back to 0, moving the hoop slowly to make the stitches close together.

For flowers like delphiniums or lupins, blocks of zigzags are worked in all directions to form a column, using a light shade in the bobbin and darker on top. Tighten the top tension to pull up the bobbin thread.

For a close-up of a poppy, use large blocks of zigzag to form the petals.

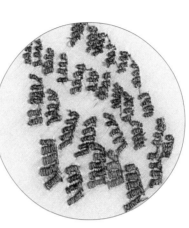

For bluebells, work small parallel rows of zigzags, diminishing in size at the top of the flower. Increase the size of the flowers towards the foreground to give perspective.

Create ferns using narrow parallel rows of zigzag at normal tension, using the same colour on top and in the bobbin. Taper the width of stitch down to 0 at the end of each frond.

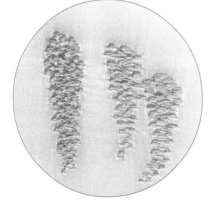

For laburnum flowers in the foreground, work blocks of zigzag reduced in size towards base of flower shape

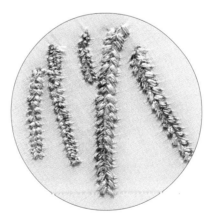

For barley, work zigzag stitch at an angle down one side and back up the other. Hold the zigzag on the spot to let the stitches build up on top of each other.

To create larger leaves work two sections of zigzag, either in the same colour or using two different shades.

Seaside garden

The areas of painted detail in this picture provide an effective contrast to the flowers and foliage. Lots of practice is needed for the technique featured, which uses zigzag stitch worked in varying width along the length of the leaves in the foreground.

Actual size

Spring Woodland

Unusually, the trees in the distance are zigzagged, which on this larger scale works well. The moss gives the foreground trees so much texture, and to recreate this I have used a straight stitch with a tight top tension, which has pulled the yellow bobbin thread to the surface to create the highlight. Actual size

52

Autumn canal

Before you begin your first project, you need to know how to stretch the silk on a frame. This keeps the material flat, square and raised from your work surface so the dye can flow without obstruction across its surface.

I always use a square wooden frame and a piece of fabric large enough for several embroideries, so I can paint more than one background at a time, and this method is detailed below.

If you are using smaller pieces of silk, or only want to prepare one background at a time, you can stretch the fabric in an embroidery hoop. The size of this project, 102 x 153mm (4 x 6in), means it will fit comfortably into a standard hoop.

There are several ways to transfer your design to the silk. If you have the confidence, you can draw freehand straight on to the surface with resist, or use an air-soluble marker pen followed by resist. If not, you may be able to place your photograph directly under the silk and trace the basic elements of the design. If you do this, use an air-soluble pen because resist will seep through the silk and mark your photograph. If the design does not show sufficiently through the silk, use tracing paper.

To section the silk, make a small cut in the selvedge and tear, very quickly, straight across the fabric. This will always give a straight edge.

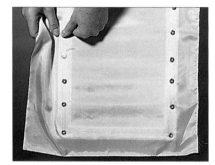

1. Lay a piece of silk over the frame. Starting at the centre, pin one edge with silk pins, which have three prongs to help them grip the material securely. Spacing the pins evenly, and pulling the silk gently as you go, work along the opposite edge.

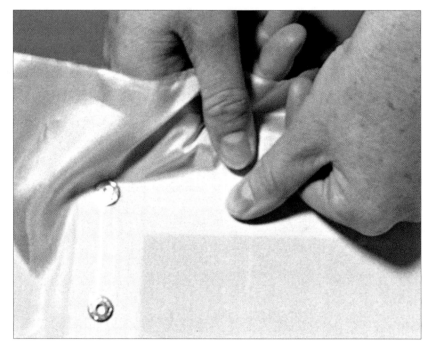

2. Work along the two remaining sides, keeping the silk square to the frame and at an even tension. Make sure you leave a little play in the silk to avoid pull lines.

3. Using a rule and an air-soluble marker pen, draw a rectangle 102 x 153mm (4 x 6in) on the silk. Placing it in the corner is more economical with the silk, and you should be able to fit another embroidery in the opposite corner. At this stage, you could paint two backgrounds the same and use one to practise stitch techniques on.

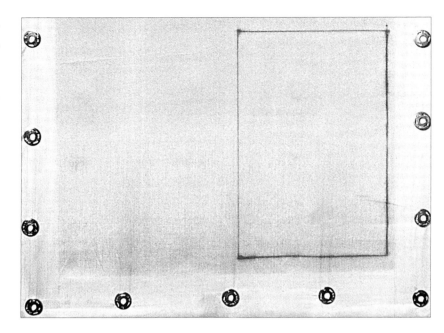

4. Referring to the source photograph above, transfer the key elements of the design to the silk with an air-soluble pen. Take care not to draw solid shapes in the area where the light shines through the branches. Make the tree shapes smaller; you can extend the size with stitches, and the tree shape will look more delicate if sky is visible through the branches.

5. Apply the resist carefully over the pen lines, keeping a constant pressure on the nib to endure consistent line thickness.

6. Add extra touches of resist for finer details, and to retain the white silk in places, such as the area in the water of the canal. Allow to dry. Hold the silk up to the light to check that there are no breaks in the lines of resist where dye could seep through.

7. Mix up the colours of silk paint you want to use, making sure you have enough to complete each section. Test the colours at the edge of your work, avoiding the wood of the frame, and remembering that they will dry lighter. Put a piece of white paper behind your work when testing colours, to ensure that they appear true. With a No. 5 brush, begin to apply the paint to the larger areas.

Note
If you want the dyes to blend into each other, do not allow one colour to dry on the fabric before adding the next.

8. Fill in areas which will be stitched with washes in appropriate colours. Leave the area of silk which will represent the sky unpainted, as the white silk will produce a pale autumnal effect.

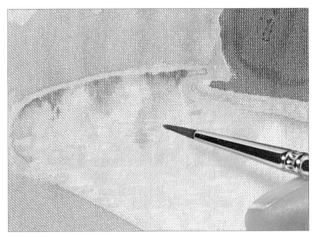

9. Mix up a palette of dye colours for the water and test at the side of the picture. With a No. 0 brush begin to paint the reflections at the far bank of the canal, omitting the barges seen in the source photo.

10. Complete the reflections in the water using a range of colours and a No. 0 brush. Keeping all brush strokes small and horizontal, start with the palest tone and work through all the colours to the darkest. Let each colour dry before applying the next − this gives you more control and allows you achieve small, fine lines of dye. Remove the silk from the frame and use a hot iron to fix the image, then wash it in hot, soapy water to remove the resist. Rinse in clear water, then iron the silk dry to ensure there are no creases.

Choosing your threads

When the painted background is complete, you can choose the threads needed for the embroidery.

Starting in the distance, analyse the colours you can see in the row of trees on the left bank of the canal. Hold the reel of thread over the photograph to double-check that it is the correct colour. Move from section to section, repeating the process. Put all the threads aside, in groups, making notes of which is intended for each area if you think it will help.

For each section you need to decide the colour, direction and type of stitch to create the effect you want. Small stitches in the distance help to create a sense of depth; this means moving the hoop slowly. Larger stitches in the foreground – such as zigzag or long, straight stitches – will bring details forward and give more perspective to the picture. The logical order of work is from the distance to the foreground, and areas which will be overlapped should be completed first.

Start with the dark tones at the base of a shape, then progress to mid-tones and finally to highlights. Remember that changing only the top thread will help to blend the colours.

When embroidering an area which includes several colours, remember to leave space for the threads and colours still to come. For example, if there are four colours in an area, the first colour should cover no more than 25 per cent of the area, or it will become overworked and too dense to stitch.

Turning the source photograph upside down can help you to focus on colours and shapes, rather than a familiar scene. Making a black-and-white photocopy of your source photograph can help you work out the tonal values without the complication of colour.

11. In good daylight and using your source photograph for reference, select the threads you plan to use in your embroidery.

Note
Before you begin, remember to bind the hoop with cotton tape so it grips the fabric well.

12. Position the silk face up over the outer hoop of an embroidery frame. Insert the inner hoop and push carefully into place. Tighten the screw on the outer hoop and pull the fabric between the two hoops until taut, taking care not to distort your picture.

13. Thread the machine with mid-green on top and dark green in the bobbin. Starting at the most distant point, embroider the base of the trees. Tighten the top tension to pull up the bobbin thread so you can see two colours, which helps the blending effect. Move the hoop slowly to produce small stitches, using a straight stitch and a tight spiralling action.

14. Embroider the pale foliage in the distance using mid-green in the bobbin and lighter green on top. Change the top thread to yellow and add more detail above the previous stitches.

15. Change to mid-brown in the bobbin and light beige on top to complete the distant foliage.

16. Starting with the darkest areas and using dark green on top and in the bobbin, begin to fill in the large area of foliage. These are the negative shapes you need to identify to give the picture form.

17. Referring to the photograph, move on to the mid-tones of the foliage and fill in the greens with appropriate threads, overlapping the dark tones to blend it together.

18. At the same time, begin to build up the grass at the side of the water using the same shades of thread and small horizontal straight stitches.

19. Change to pale green on top and yellow in the bobbin and begin to add the lighter tones in the foreground foliage.

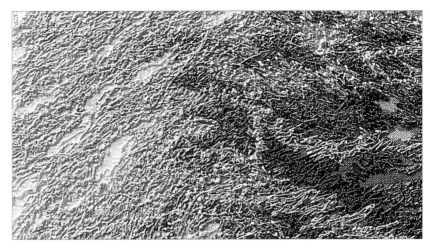

20. Embroider the background tones of the tree using pale yellow in the bobbin and pale peach on top, in straight stitches following the direction of the foliage. Leave spaces for colours to come, and to let the sky show through.

21. Using progressively deeper tones of the same combination of top and bobbin threads, continue to build up the foliage on the tree on the left, overlapping the tones to build up the 3D effect.

22. With dark grey on the top and in the bobbin, use a small straight stitch to put in the far edge of the canal bank. Change to lighter grey on top and in the bobbin for the distance. Complete the grass border on the far bank using mid-green in the bobbin and cinnamon on top. With a variety of autumn tones, 'draw' in the fallen leaves on the bank.

23. Put in the branches using a straight stitch with mid-grey on top and mid-brown in the bobbin. Stop the machine to move from one area to another, and cut the trailing threads later.

24. Using mid-green on top and in the bobbin, put in horizontal bands of straight stitches for the darker tones of foreground grass.

25. Finish by filling in the gaps with blue green in the bobbin and paler green on top.

Autumn canal
This picture was worked completely in straight stitch.
Actual size

The canal

*In this variation of a canal scene, the painted reflections are
an important part of the design. I started painting with the
palest tones and progressed through mid-tones to the darkest,
waiting patiently for each colour to dry before applying the
next. I drew some horizontal broken lines on the water with
resist to retain some white in the reflections, and this also
helped to control the flow of the dye.*

Actual size

Woodland daffodils

This project uses a limited number of stitch techniques. The composition has three basic sections: the woodland in the background; the trees in the middle distance and the drifts of daffodils. The selection of threads reflects this: a range of browns for the trees and woodland; a range of greens for the daffodil foliage, and a range of yellows for the flower heads. The background is a good example of blending tones of the same colour. The technique may seem complicated at first, but as you become more practised it will seem automatic.

The trees in the middle distance are embroidered with parallel rows of straight stitch along the length of the trunk. The drifts of daffodils are a combination of straight stitch for the foliage and small zigzags for the flower heads. The individual daffodils in the foreground are worked in a large zigzag stitch in three shades of yellow.

The logical progression of work is from the distance to the foreground, with the scale of stitches increasing toward the front to create a sense of depth and perspective.

1. Mask off the area of the source photograph you intend to use for your composition.

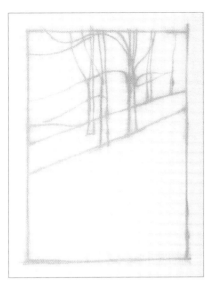

2. Stretch the silk on a wooden frame with silk pins – see page 54. Referring to the source photograph, draw in the four basic areas of the design and mark in the position of the trees. Use an air-soluble pen, then draw the outlines in with resist.

3. When the resist is dry, paint the background washes in shades of green and brown.

4. Start your embroidery with the distant woodland, lining up the threads selected before you begin. With a very dark brown thread in the bobbin and on top, embroider the lower part of the wooded area, using small straight stitches in diagonal lines to suggest the direction of the branches. Work densely at the base and more openly higher up, leaving spaces for the tree trunks and for stitching in the mid and light tones, which will be added next.

5. Still with dark brown in the bobbin and with the next (lighter) shade on top, continue building up the background. Fill in the spaces left between the darkest stitches then work higher, leaving gaps between the stitches. Fill the bobbin with the shade used on top in the previous stage and put the next lighter shade on top. Repeat until all the brown tones have been used, finishing with the two lightest for the highlights.

6. Turn the picture upside-down to analyse the shapes of the dark tones in the flowers. Embroider them using straight stitch, using dark green thread on top and in the bobbin.

7. Change to mid-green on top and in the bobbin. Overlap some of the dark green stitching, and fill in the area between. Be aware of the position of the daffodil flowers and leave spaces for them.

66

8. With pale yellow in the bobbin and a darker yellow on top, put in the impression of drifts of daffodils among the trees. Use a small zigzag stitch and move the hoop horizontally. Tighten the top tension until you can see both colours on the surface.

9. With running stitch and dark brown on top and in the bobbin, put in the strong shadows down the side of the tree trunks and on the main branches.

10. Continue with the trunks of the trees using parallel rows of straight stitch in olive green, then mid-brown and finally beige for the highlights.

11. Using the daffodil yellow top and bottom, put in a strong row of closely-worked zigzags to represent the massed flowers on the brow of the bank.

12. With the same technique and combination of threads, complete several rows of randomly-distributed flowers. These should be placed in the spaces in the foliage, moving the hoop in a horizontal direction.

13. Still using the daffodil yellow on top and in the bobbin, add the daffodils in the foreground using slightly larger zigzag stitches. Work the flowers in drifts in a horizontal direction. Snip any trailing threads that connect individual daffodils.

14. Change the top thread to a slightly deeper yellow and fill in the centres of the daffodils.

16. With the picture virtually complete, it is a good idea to take a critical look at the tonal and compositional balance as something usually needs adjusting. In this case, the bank on the right looks too pale, and the road seems too dominant a feature.

15. With mid-green thread on top and in the bobbin, add the last details to the daffodil foliage using straight stitch. This can be used to re-define the shapes of the flower heads.

The finished embroidery

The starkness of the area of bank has been reduced by embroidering it with horizontal straight stitches using light brown. I could have re-painted the area in a stronger colour but I felt that it also needed texture.
The shape of the road has been changed by adding more stitches to the background behind the trees with the dark brown that was used for the original section.

Actual size

View from my window
The zigzag used for the tree trunks stands out well from the horizontal straight lines used for the frosty grass in the distance. The pale blue threads used to give the effect of frost are in the bobbin, pulled up by a tight top tension to give colour and texture to the stitch.

Actual size

Dappled shadows

Overlapping rows of zigzag stitch give the shading to these tree trunks and branches. The path was painted with a pale wash, and when it was dry the shadows were painted with a fine (size 0) brush.

Actual size

Flower border

This is a project with a wide variety of stitch techniques, although it is simple in its composition.

For this picture, you need to be able to identify the negative shapes, for example the dark tones in the foliage. Drawing in the flower heads (the positive shapes) helps with this. It is important to remember to leave spaces in the embroidery for fine details such as the flower heads. If an area is over-stitched, it is difficult to embroider with accuracy.

Turn the hoop sideways to work on the gravel path. You will find that the hoop is easier to move vertically than horizontally, and with better control you will be able to 'draw' the gravel more successfully. In this example, the path has been simplified and embroidered with only a limited number of colours. If you prefer, you can add more detail as gravel comes in many shades and colours.

The source photograph and the threads selected.

1. Select the area of the source photograph you want to use for your composition.

2. With an air-soluble pen, draw an outline of the composition. Apply resist to all the lines.

3. Wash in green tones for the foliage and the small triangle of lawn in the foreground. Put in a pale beige wash for the steps and path. When dry, add a deeper shade for the shadows across the steps in the distance. Using grey on top and in the bobbin, put in the shadows under the step and at the edge of the gravel path, under the flowers.

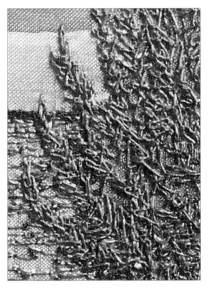

4. Using the same grey in the bobbin and a paler grey on top, begin to fill in the gravel path with random straight stitches. Wiggle the hoop a little to avoid straight lines – they should lie in a horizontal direction.

5. Using brown on top and darker brown in the bobbin, put in the woody lavender stems. Change to green and complete the foliage with a straight stitch, zigzagged by hand along the length of the stem.

6. Mark out the position of the large osteospermum flowers. This can be done with permanent marker pen, as it will be covered by embroidery. Marking the positions will help you to embroider the negative shapes around the flowers.

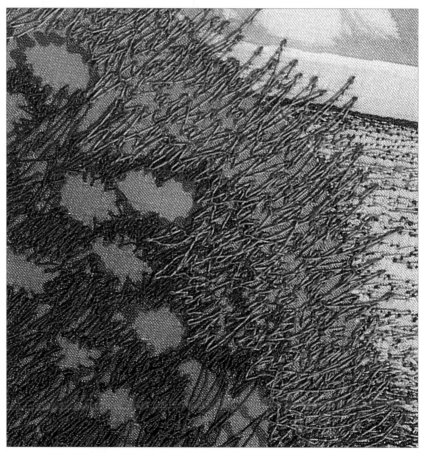

7. With very dark green thread on top and in the bobbin, machine in the background around the flower heads. Use straight stitch but direct it diagonally with a slight curve.

8. With straight stitch and using mid-green in the bobbin and sage green on top, machine in the foliage of the aubrieta behind the osteospermums. Use small stitches to create distance.

74

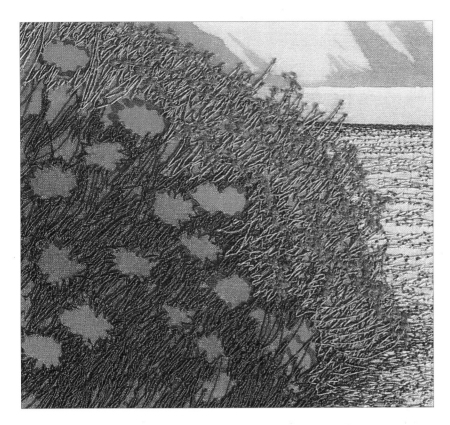

8. With a narrow zigzag stitch and using deep pink on top and in the bobbin, machine in the heads of the flowers.

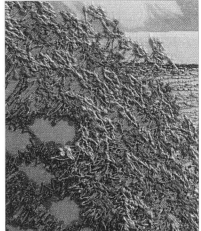

10. Change to mid pink in the bobbin and pale pink on top and complete the details of the aubrieta flowers.

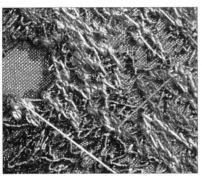

11. When moving between areas of stitching which are the same colour, carry the thread over the work and snip the trailing thread later to separate the groups of flowers – see page 41 for details of the method.

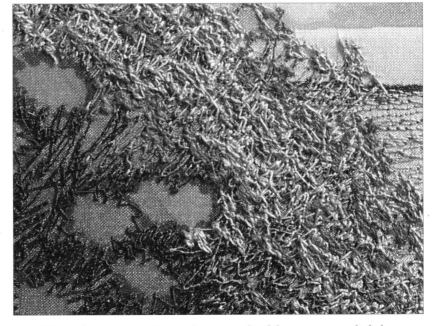

12. With a straight stitch, run between the foliage using a slightly lighter green on top and a very light green in the bobbin to put in the highlights, and to separate the flower heads a little.

13. With straight stitch and using two different shades of green, put in foliage between the gaps left for the osteospermums.

14. With white on top and in the bobbin for some flowers and white in the bobbin and lilac on top for others, put in the petals using a wide zigzag stitch. As each petal is completed, rotate the hoop slightly and work the next, so they fan out from the centre.

15. With deep pink in the bobbin and yellow on top, with a small zigzag stitch worked on the spot, put in the centres of the osteospermum flowers. Use a small zigzag stitch for the petals of the small white snow-in-summer (ceratium tomentosum) flowers. Change to pale pink and add the final details of the aubrieta where it breaks through between the other flowers.

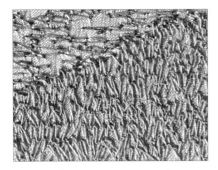

16. With green on top and in the bobbin, use rows of straight stitches to embroider the triangle of lawn.

17. With very pale blue-green on top and in the bobbin, put in a few random straight stitches at the base of the border, which will add highlights to the foliage and have the effect of separating the small white flowers. Check the balance of the composition and adjust if necessary.

Leading to the greenhouse
Actual size

The artist's garden

My garden is an endless source of inspiration. I used artistic licence to replace a plant that had finished flowering with osteospermums. The scale of stitching is important: small straight stitches and tiny zigzag stitches were used for the delphiniums, roses and the alchemilla mollis in the background. The stronger, bolder zigzag treatment and the increase in scale of the penstemon and osteospermum in the foreground adds depth.

Actual size

The Rose Arch

The path is a mixture of painted shadows and straight stitch to emphasise the paving stones. This leads your eye into the picture through a wide range of greenery and foliage to the sunlight beyond the gate. Zigzag stitch has been used in the foreground to give larger-scale leaves and flowers. The distant foliage is a tiny straight stitch.

Actual size

Index